UNITED KINGDOM

Written by
Peter Evans

Illustrated by
Nila Aye, Hardlines and Michael Munday

Edited by
Caroline White

Designed by
Clare Davey

Picture research by
Helen Taylor

CONTENTS

Introducing the United Kingdom

The United Kingdom is made up of England, Scotland, Wales and the province of Northern Ireland. It covers nearly 250 000 square kilometres and is approximately 1000 kilometres (600 miles) from north to south.

Britain is made up of England, Scotland and Wales. It is surrounded by sea and is the eighth largest island in the world. The British Isles are made up of Britain and the whole of Ireland, including the Republic of Ireland.

The United Kingdom (UK) is part of Europe. Its neighbours are France, across the Channel, and the Republic of Ireland.

A sandy beach on Jersey, one of the Channel Islands

Snow-capped Ben Nevis, Scotland

The most westerly point of the UK is the tiny island of Rockall out in the Atlantic Ocean. It is 300 kilometres from the Scottish mainland.

The most northerly part of the UK is the rocky island of Muckle Flugga in the Shetlands. It is closer to Norway than it is to the Scottish mainland.

Muckle Flugga

N

| 0 | | 100 km |
| 0 | 50 miles | |

The highest cliffs in the UK are 400 metres high in St Kilda in the Western Isles of Scotland.

St Kilda

The highest mountain in the UK is Ben Nevis in Scotland. It is 1343 metres high.

North Sea

Ben Nevis

SCOTLAND

The biggest inland lake in the UK is Lough Neagh in Northern Ireland. It covers 385 square kilometres.

Edinburgh

Atlantic Ocean

Some parts of the land in eastern England are below sea-level.

Lough Neagh   Belfast

N. IRELAND

REPUBLIC OF IRELAND

The most easterly part of the UK is Ness Point in Lowestoft.

ENGLAND

London is the biggest city in the UK. Seven million people live in an area of over 3000 square kilometres.

Lowestoft

R. Severn

The longest river in the UK is the River Severn. It starts in the Welsh mountains and flows for over 354 kilometres (220 miles) through England to the sea.

WALES

Cardiff

London

The Channel Islands are a few kilometres from the coast of France. They are part of the British Isles but they are not part of the UK.

The English Channel, separating England from the European mainland, is only 30 kilometres wide at its narrowest point.

English Channel

FRANCE

Channel Islands

Facts and figures

The Queen is the head of state of the United Kingdom. She inherited her position from her father, King George VI. The Queen and her relatives are called the royal family. Her picture is on all UK money and postage stamps.

Parliament

The UK is ruled by Parliament. This is made up of 650 Members of Parliament (MPs) who are elected by the people. Members of Parliament belong to different political parties. The party with the most elected MPs usually forms the government, which then decides how the country should be run. The other parties form the opposition.

Scotland and Northern Ireland have some laws which are different from England and Wales. They have different school systems too.

Queen Elizabeth II at the State Opening of Parliament

Flags

The national flag is called the Union flag, or Union Jack, and combines the flags of St George (England), St Andrew (Scotland) and St Patrick (Northern Ireland). The design does not include the Welsh flag.

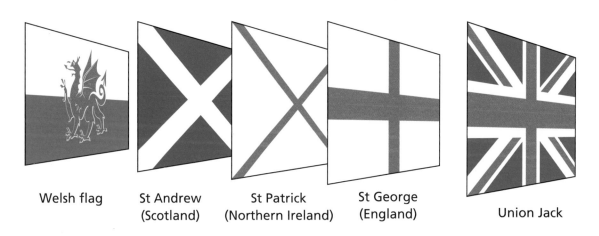

Welsh flag   St Andrew (Scotland)   St Patrick (Northern Ireland)   St George (England)   Union Jack

Population

Over 58 million people, or 1 per cent of the world's population, live in the UK. One-fifth are children under the age of sixteen. Another fifth are over the age of sixty. On average there are 240 people for every square kilometre of land.

The population is not spread out evenly. There are about 4000 people squeezed into each square kilometre in central London, and only 8 people per square kilometre in the Scottish Highlands.

Leisure

Watching TV is the most popular leisure activity in the UK. Each person views an average of 25 hours per week. People over the age of sixty watch ten hours more than this, while children under the age of sixteen watch five hours less.

The most popular free tourist attraction in the UK is Blackpool Pleasure Beach. It has six and a half million visitors a year.

Did you know?
- Around 750 000 babies are born each year in the UK and 650 000 people die.
- Nine million pupils go to 35 000 schools.
- On average women live until they are 78 years old, men until they are 75.
- Half the deaths in the UK are from heart disease, the next most are from cancer.

UK top five leisure activities
★ Watching TV

★ Listening to the radio, CDs, tapes and records

★ Reading

★ Caring for pets

★ Gardening

Land use in the UK
- agriculture
- forest
- built-up area
- mountainous and other land

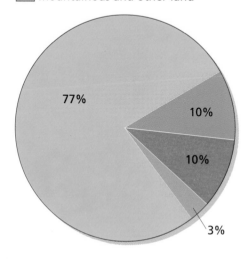

77% 10% 10% 3%

Land use

Three-quarters of the land area of the UK is used for agriculture, one-tenth is forest, another tenth is built on and the rest is mountainous or unusable.

Languages

As well as English, Gaelic is spoken in many parts of Scotland and Northern Ireland. Welsh is spoken by over half a million people in Wales. Several hundred other languages are spoken by people in the UK, including Urdu, Hindi, Punjabi, Greek, Turkish and Mandarin.

English: My name is Peter.

Welsh: Fy enw i yw Peter.

Gaelic: `Se Peadair an t-ainm a tha orm.

Urdu: Meera naam Peter hai.

People

About half the people in the United Kingdom go out to work. Two million others would like to work but can't find any. They are called unemployed. The rest of the population are children, retired or look after families at home.

Three-quarters of the UK working population work in service industries, such as offices or shops. The other quarter mostly work in the manufacturing or construction industries.

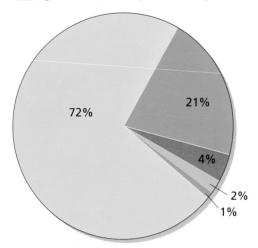

Working population of the UK

- service industries
- manufacturing
- construction
- energy and water
- agriculture, forestry and fishing

72%

21%

4%

2%

1%

'My name is Alisdair. My family and I live on a croft [small farm] on the Isle of Skye in the west of Scotland. We keep animals to help feed ourselves, and I also work at the oil terminal in the nearby town.'

'My name is Arthur and I make engines in a factory in the Midlands. More and more jobs like this are being done by machines. There will soon be less work for skilled people like me to do.'

'My name is Shahnaz and I work for an insurance company in their new offices. I only work mornings because I have to pick up my children from school.'

'My name is Paul and I'm looking for a job. No one seems to want to take on young people like me, although my girlfriend's just got a part-time job.'

'My name is Margaret [right]. I live by myself now that my husband has died. I'm quite happy as long as I can get about, although I do have to keep an eye on the money.'

'My name is Richard and I'm the managing director of a large supermarket chain. I'm retiring at the end of the year, so I'll be able spend more time at home, maybe playing a bit of golf and having a few more holidays.'

Invaders and settlers

For thousands of years people have come to the United Kingdom to invade and plunder or to stay and settle. Much of the population today is descended from people who came to these islands from many different parts of the world.

Romans

The Romans first invaded Britain in 55 BC and began to settle in AD 43. They built fortified towns and long straight roads all over England and some way into Wales and Scotland. In 122 the Romans built Hadrian's Wall, just south of the present border between England and Scotland, to defend themselves against the Celtic tribes to the north.

The word Britain comes from *Britannia*, the name given to the country by the Romans. The Romans had to leave Britain around 410 to look after other parts of their empire.

Anglo-Saxons

The Anglo-Saxons came from Northern Europe. By the year 600 they had settled most of England and set up separate kingdoms, such as Mercia, Northumbria and Wessex. Each kingdom had its own king. The most famous Anglo-Saxon king was Alfred the Great. He ruled Wessex from 871 to 899. The Anglo-Saxons did not venture into Wales, Scotland, Ireland or the most distant parts of Cornwall.

800 Vikings settle in Orkney Islands and Shetland Islands

122 Hadrian's Wall built

840 Vikings settle in Dublin

York

Chester

Warwick

Pembroke

London

Southampton

Routes taken by invaders and settlers

Romans
Anglo-Saxons
Vikings
Normans

1066 Normans led by Duke William

55 BC Romans led by Julius Caesar

Romans begin to settle		Romans defeated by Anglo-Saxon army			Viking Great Army invades	William the Conqueror invades from France	Normans control South Wales
43		376			866	1066	1100

		878	1086	1171
		King Alfred keeps Vikings to the east of England	Domesday Book records landownership	Henry II invades Ireland

Vikings

The first Viking invaders came from Scandinavia in 793. Vikings from Norway settled in the north and west of the Scottish mainland and in the Scottish islands. The Great Army of Vikings from Denmark landed and settled in the east of England. King Alfred of Wessex defeated the Great Army in many battles and stopped them moving any further west. Some went on round the south coast and settled in parts of South Wales, eastern Ireland and northern France.

Normans

The Normans were descended from Vikings who had settled in France. In 1066 Duke William of Normandy invaded England and claimed the throne. In the years that followed he set up a powerful government and built castles to control the country. Many of the castles were built in Wales, where he had trouble with the rebellious Welsh princes. The Normans were the last invaders to come to the UK.

The English, Scots and Welsh continued to attack each other for many years. In 1171 King Henry II of England invaded Ireland and became King of Ireland too. In 1284 Edward I defeated the Welsh and became king of all three countries.

793 Viking raids begin

400 Anglo-Saxon raids begin

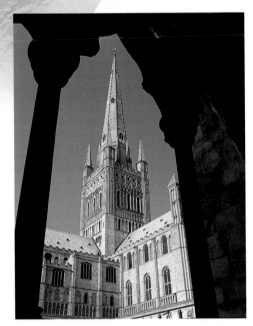

Norwich Cathedral was founded by the Normans in 1096.

Changing language

Each group of invaders brought their own words into the English language.

• Nearly half the English words used today come from Latin, the language of the Romans.

• Place-names ending in '-ham', '-ing' and '-ton' are Anglo-Saxon.

• Viking words include 'happy', 'ugly' and 'law'.

• The Normans introduced French words into the English language, such as 'cul-de-sac'.

Famous monarchs

In 1485 Henry VII became the first English king from the Tudor family. He made peace treaties with neighbouring countries – France, Spain and Scotland – so that trade could prosper.

The Tudors

Henry VII's son, Henry VIII, ruled from 1509 to 1547. In that time he made himself head of the Church of England, closed all convents and monasteries, went to war with France and had six wives. He was desperate to have a son to succeed him as King, but it was his daughter who was to become one of the most famous English monarchs.

Henry's daughter, Elizabeth I, ruled for nearly fifty years (1558–1603). Art and music flourished during her reign, and English sailors explored the seas and traded all over the world. They also plundered and stole from Spanish ships and colonies. In 1588 the King of Spain decided to send an armada of ships to attack England. The Spanish Armada, however, was defeated by the English fleet and the stormy weather.

Elizabeth I had no children. When she died in 1603, King James VI of Scotland also became King James I of England.

Sixteenth-century portrait of Henry VIII

The Tudors ruled England, Wales and parts of Ireland, but Scotland had its own kings, many of whom came to the throne while they were still children. James IV (1488–1513) was fifteen years old when he became King, James V (1513–42) was seventeen months old, while James VI (1567–1625) was thirteen months old.

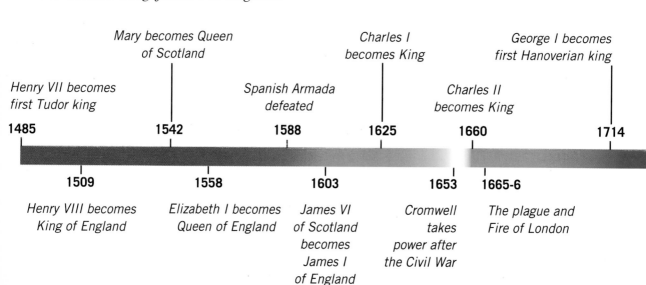

Mary becomes Queen of Scotland

Charles I becomes King

George I becomes first Hanoverian king

Henry VII becomes first Tudor king

Spanish Armada defeated

Charles II becomes King

1485   1542   1588   1625   1660   1714

1509   1558   1603   1653   1665-6

Henry VIII becomes King of England

Elizabeth I becomes Queen of England

James VI of Scotland becomes James I of England

Cromwell takes power after the Civil War

The plague and Fire of London

Portrait of Elizabeth I standing on a map of England

Mary Queen of Scots

Mary Queen of Scots (1542–67) was only seven days old when she became the first Queen of Scotland. She went on to become Queen of France as well. There were many battles between the English and Scots during her reign.

Queen Victoria

Queen Victoria is the UK's longest reigning monarch. During her reign (1837–1901) the UK became a powerful industrial force. Towns and cities grew, with houses for working people, factories, mills and shipyards being built. The Victorians also built railways, and gas and electric lighting became available. Sewage systems and clean water supplies were installed and there were improvements in health and medicine.

Throughout Queen Victoria's reign, many people in Ireland campaigned to become an independent country. Eventually, in 1921, Ireland was divided up into the independent Republic of Ireland in the south and Northern Ireland in the north, which was to remain part of the UK.

Queen Victoria and the Scots Guards, 1895

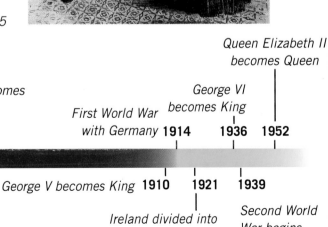

Victoria becomes Queen **1837**

First World War with Germany **1914**

George VI becomes King **1936**

Queen Elizabeth II becomes Queen **1952**

1801 Ireland becomes part of the United Kingdom

George V becomes King **1910**

Ireland divided into Northern Ireland and the Republic of Ireland **1921**

Second World War begins **1939**

Weather and climate

The weather in the United Kingdom is not particularly hot, cold, wet or dry. This kind of mild weather with few extremes is called a temperate climate. One thing the UK weather is famous for is the way that it changes from one day to the next.

N

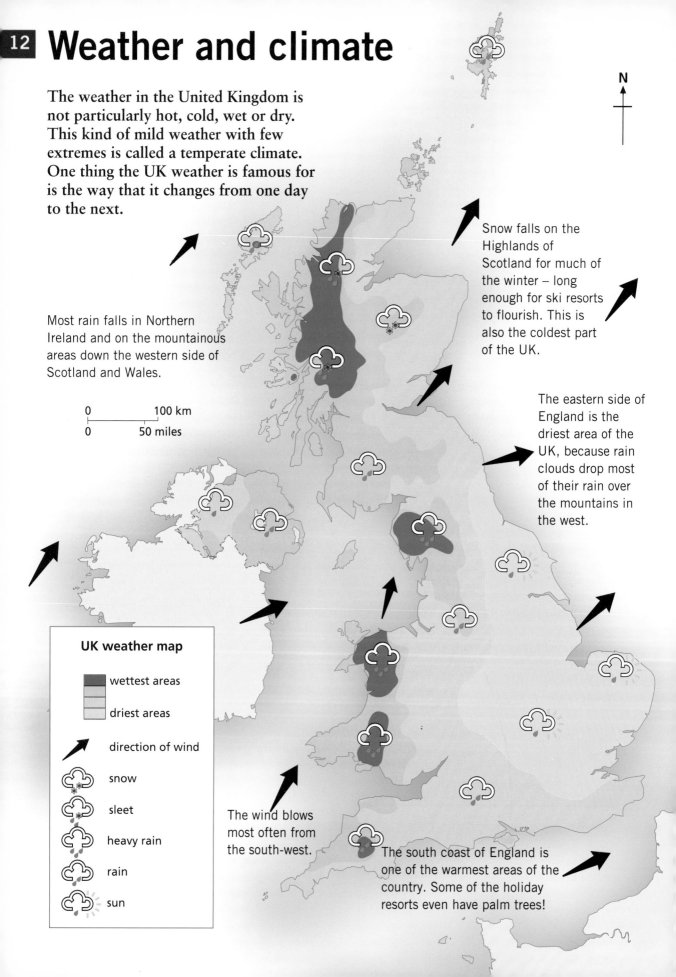

Most rain falls in Northern Ireland and on the mountainous areas down the western side of Scotland and Wales.

Snow falls on the Highlands of Scotland for much of the winter – long enough for ski resorts to flourish. This is also the coldest part of the UK.

The eastern side of England is the driest area of the UK, because rain clouds drop most of their rain over the mountains in the west.

| 0 | | 100 km |
| 0 | | 50 miles |

UK weather map

- wettest areas
- driest areas
- ➤ direction of wind
- snow
- sleet
- heavy rain
- rain
- sun

The wind blows most often from the south-west.

The south coast of England is one of the warmest areas of the country. Some of the holiday resorts even have palm trees!

*Children from Oak Farm
School in London carry out a
weather project.*

Weather project

If you want to get a good idea of how the weather changes, you can set up your own weather project at home or school. To get the full picture, you will need to measure the temperature, rainfall and wind direction every day for a year. The UK weather changes so much that if you only measure it for a week or so, you will get a misleading result.

If you have not got the time or the equipment to do the measuring yourself, you can get temperature and rainfall figures from daily newspaper weather reports.

*Daily newspaper weather
report for the UK*

c, cloudy; f, fair, fg, fog; hz, haze,; r, rain; sn, snow; s, sunny; sh, showers; th, thunder

		°C °F												
Aberdeen	r	20 68	Brighton	c	19 66	Exeter	c	21 70	Liverpool	s	25 77	Ronaldsway	s	21 70
Anglesey	s	22 72	Bristol	c	22 72	Glasgow	c	20 68	Lizard	c	20 68	Scarborough	f	21 70
Ayr	c	20 68	Cardiff	f	23 73	Guernsey	c	17 63	London	sh	20 68	Southampton	sh	20 68
Belfast	f	23 73	Carlisle	f	24 75	Inverness	f	19 66	Manchester	s	25 77	Southend	c	21 70
Birmingham	c	21 70	Dover	dr	18 64	Ipswich	c	22 72	Newcastle	f	22 72	Stornoway	r	16 61
Blackpool	s	25 77	Dublin	s	23 73	Isles of Scilly	c	19 66	Oxford	sh	21 70	Tiree	s	18 64
Bournemouth	dr	19 66	Edinburgh	dr	18 64	Jersey	m	16 61	Plymouth	f	21 70	York	s	25 77

Freak weather

The United Kingdom can get sudden extremes of weather, although extreme weather in one part of the country may be considered normal somewhere else. Strong winds and deep snow that cause damage and chaos in the south of England are more common in the north of Scotland and cause fewer problems.

In the Great Winter of 1607 large rivers, such as the Thames in England and the Firth of Forth in Scotland, froze over. People were able to walk and drive carts across the ice. They even held 'frost fairs' and set up stalls and side-shows on the ice. Ships became trapped as the sea froze around the coast.

In the winter of 1947 it was very cold throughout the UK. Thick snow brought train and road traffic to a standstill. In some places the snow stayed on the ground until April. People suffered because there was a shortage of coal for fires following the Second World War.

Digging a car out of a snowdrift in Hertfordshire, 1947

A seventeenth-century 'frost fair' on the River Thames, London

Millions of trees were destroyed by strong winds on 16 October 1987.

In 1953 high tides and strong winds caused the sea to break through the sea walls along the east coast of England. Thousands of square miles of low-lying land were flooded. Three hundred people died and thirty thousand were made homeless.

In 1976 there was a drought during the hottest summer on record. In many parts of the UK no rain fell for over forty days. Reservoirs ran dry and green fields turned brown.

On the night of 16 October 1987 a great storm swept across southern England, destroying over fifteen million trees and killing nineteen people. Had the storm happened during the day, many more people would have died. Wind speeds of over a hundred miles an hour were recorded as chimneys blew down and caravans and boats were tossed up into the air.

A dried-up reservoir in the summer of 1976

Seas and coastlines

The United Kingdom coastline measures over 15 000 kilometres (9300 miles) and ranges from towering cliffs to sandy beaches. Nearly a quarter of the coastline of England and Wales is protected by artificial sea walls to stop the sea washing away the land.

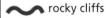

Coastlines around the UK

~~ rocky cliffs

~ lowland, sandy dunes and estuaries

⫽⫽ protective sea walls

Around the UK coast the sea rises and falls by about 4.5 metres as the tide goes in and out.

What differences can you see between high tide (top picture) and low tide (bottom picture) at St Ives in Cornwall?

The highest cliffs in the UK are 400 metres high in St Kilda in the Western Isles of Scotland.

In the North Sea giant floating rigs drill down below the sea bed and send supplies of gas and oil back to the mainland.

Stretches of the east coast of England are so soft they are washed away by the sea. Several metres of land can collapse into the sea at a time, sometimes taking houses, roads and trees with it.

The fallen material is carried away by the sea and eventually deposited further along the coast as mud flats or beaches.

The Giant's Causeway on the coast of Northern Ireland is made of huge six-sided blocks of volcanic rock.

Along the west coast of Scotland, Wales and the South-West of England are cliffs made of hard rock. These are difficult for the sea to wear away.

The White Cliffs of Dover are made of chalk. They are one of the UK's most famous views.

Follow a river

The River Severn is the longest river in the United Kingdom. It starts up in the Plynlimon mountains in central Wales and flows for 354 kilometres (220 miles) through England to the sea.

As the river widens, it goes through the small market towns of Newtown and Welshpool. In this hilly area main roads and a railway line share the river valley.

Welshpool

The River Severn is fed by rain falling on the Welsh mountains. The river starts by flowing east and then north – away from the sea. Other tributaries join it from the surrounding hills.

Newtown

The first cast iron bridge in the world crosses the River Severn at Ironbridge.

WALES

Stourport is now a centre for canal and river-cruising holidays.

In the Severn Estuary the rise and fall of the tide is the greatest in the UK – around 12.5 metres. There have been plans to build a tidal barrage to harness the power of the waves and generate electricity.

Cardiff

ENGLAND

Crossing the border into England, the land becomes flatter and the river begins to meander through quiet countryside.

The first big town on the Severn is Shrewsbury. It was built in a loop of the river in the thirteenth century as a fortress town to defend the English border against the Welsh.

Shrewsbury

Ironbridge

At Ironbridge, near Telford, the Severn passes through a narrow gorge. This is the site of many early industries and the world's first cast iron bridge, built in 1779.

Stourport

The river turns south and gets wider. It can now be used for transport. Lock-gates allow barges and boats to pass through.

Worcester

Stourport was once a busy inland port with warehouses and quays. It was built where the canal from Birmingham joins the River Severn.

Tewkesbury

The Severn continues south through Worcester and Tewkesbury towards Gloucester. This stretch of the river often floods and there are water meadows either side to allow this to happen.

Gloucester

A cathedral and busy inland port were built at Gloucester, the lowest point at which the river could be crossed.

M4

Bristol

After Gloucester the Severn becomes tidal and gets wider still. The estuary is now crossed by two motorway bridges and a railway tunnel. The second road-crossing is the longest bridge in the UK.

At certain times of the year, when conditions are right, a tidal wave called the Severn Bore rushes up the river. The bore can measure up to 2 metres high. Sometimes people ride it on surfboards and in small boats.

Farming

Three-quarters of the land in the United Kingdom is used for farming. Only one in fifty people work in agriculture, but they grow nearly half the food that we eat.

In hilly and moorland areas, such as the Scottish Highlands, Welsh hills and English Pennines, sheep are farmed for their wool. On the lower slopes cattle are reared for beef.

In recent years farmers have started growing new crops. These have changed the look of the countryside. In the summer, oil seed rape has bright yellow flowers and a strong sweet smell. It is used to make cooking oil and fuel. Some people do not like it because the pollen gives them hay fever.

In the drier eastern side of the country large arable farms grow wheat and barley. These crops are harvested using the latest machinery. Potatoes and other vegetables are grown where the soil is richer.

In the south and west of the country dairy cattle are farmed for their milk. The milk is made into cream, butter, cheese and yoghurt. The wetter weather produces more grass for the cattle to eat.

N

0   100 km
0   50 miles

Types of farm

 beef cattle

dairy cattle

 sheep

orchards and market gardening

 cereals

In some sheltered areas fruit and vegetables are grown in market gardens.

There are 7.5 million pigs, 11 million cattle, 44 million sheep and 92 million chickens in the UK. Farmers grow 15 million tonnes of wheat, 9 million tonnes of sugar beet and 8 million tonnes of potatoes. They also produce 14 thousand million litres of milk – that's nearly 250 litres for each person in the UK.

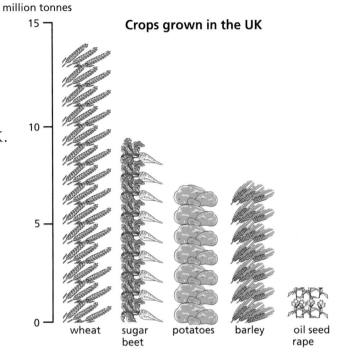

Crops grown in the UK

million tonnes

(bar chart showing crop production in million tonnes: wheat ≈15, sugar beet ≈9, potatoes ≈8, barley ≈7, oil seed rape ≈1)

Many animals, such as chickens, are bred indoors for us to eat. This is called factory farming.

Change in diet

Compared with ten years ago, people in the UK eat far less sugar, less fatty food, less meat and fewer eggs. We eat fewer fresh vegetables but more fresh fruit. More non-dairy spreads and low-fat oils are used. Fifty per cent of milk is now semi-skimmed.

The yellow oil seed rape flowers die and turn brown before the seeds are harvested.

Industry

One hundred years ago the United Kingdom was famous for its heavy industries. Mines, shipyards, steelworks, factories and mills used coal and steam power to make products that were exported all over the world. They also employed millions of people.

South Wales was well known for its coal. Glasgow, Newcastle and Belfast were renowned for shipbuilding. Irish linen and cutlery 'Made in Sheffield' were famous all over the world.

This has all changed in recent years. Today it is often cheaper to buy things from other countries than make them in the UK. Many more people now work in offices than in factories.

In 1955 there were 850 working coal mines in the UK. In 1992 there were 50. In 1995 there were 27. There are hardly any shipyards left in Newcastle and Glasgow, and there are only a few steelworks in Sheffield and cotton mills in Lancashire.

Old factories in industrial cities such as Sheffield are knocked down to make way for new offices and superstores.

Service industries

Many industries do not make things but provide a service to other people. They include shops, offices, warehouses, banks, garages, restaurants, local government, schools and tourism. Service industries employ nearly three-quarters of the working population. Because of modern communications, such as motorways, phone lines and computer links, they do not have to be in big towns or cities where the old factories used to be.

Some old industries have survived, such as pottery-making in Stoke-on-Trent. They employ fewer people than before. Cars continue to be manufactured in the UK, but they are now made in new factories owned by Japanese companies. There is still some shipbuilding in Belfast, and one-third of UK steel continues to be made in Wales.

In some places new industries have replaced the old. There are now more electronics factories in Scotland than anywhere else in the UK. Some of the most successful manufacturing industries are those that make food and drink.

There is an increasing demand for materials that come from the ground. Stone quarries provide the raw materials for road building, water purification, concrete manufacture, chemical fertilisers, and even toothpaste.

Sand and gravel are also dug from the ground, as is clay, the raw material for making pottery, tiles and bricks.

Limestone quarry in the Mendip Hills, Somerset

Expanding industries include those that manufacture packaged foods.

UK top five manufacturing industries

★ Food and drink

★ Electrical goods

★ Chemicals

★ Paper and printing

★ Machinery

Transport

The United Kingdom is small with lots of people who want to travel about and send their goods from place to place. There is an efficient transport system, with over 360 000 kilometres (225 000 miles) of roads and 16 500 kilometres (10 000 miles) of railway tracks.

Motorways make up only 1 per cent of the road mileage but carry 15 per cent of the traffic. In the past ten years the number of journeys that people make in the UK has gone up by over a third. On average each person travels over 10 000 kilometres (6000 miles) a year. Nearly nine-tenths of all passenger journeys are made by car.

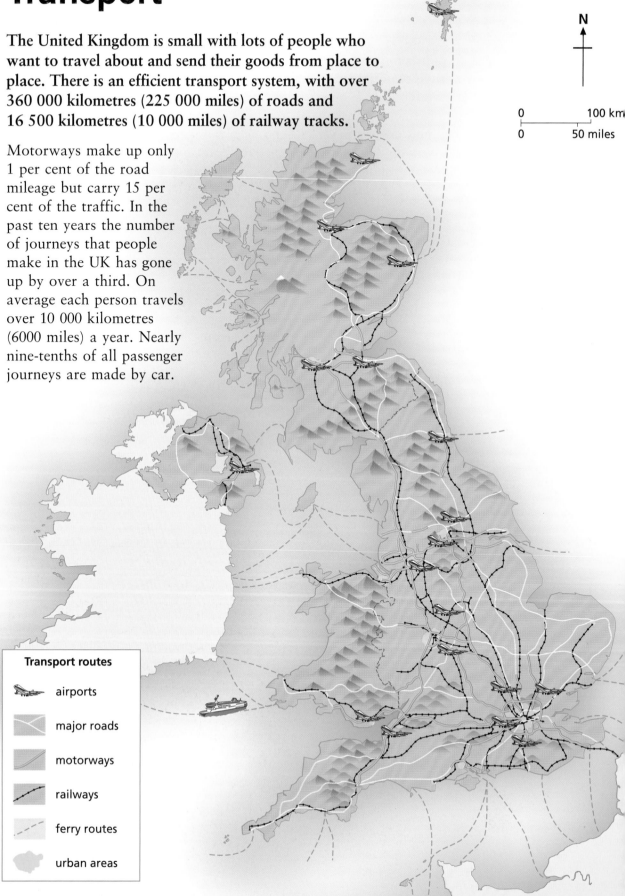

N

| 0 | 100 km |
| 0 | 50 miles |

Transport routes

✈	airports
	major roads
	motorways
	railways
	ferry routes
	urban areas

Trucks

About half of all UK goods traffic travels by road. It is now so easy for traffic to get about that trucks can deliver goods hundreds of miles around the country from warehouses near the motorways.

Trucks drive through the night, delivering goods from the warehouse to the customer.

Minibuses carry passengers around the city of Cardiff.

Manchester has a modern tram network running through the city centre.

Percentage of passenger journeys made in the UK

- 1% planes
- 6% trains
- 6% buses, coaches
- 87% cars, taxis, motorbikes

Public transport

There are now more buses in towns, but many of them are smaller and so carry fewer passengers. People in the country rely on cars to get about because train and bus services have been cut back over recent years.

The public transport system in London is widely used because it is difficult to drive and park in the capital. Some cities, such as Manchester and Newcastle, have modern light railway networks that go through the city centre. They encourage people to leave their cars at home.

Sea and air

Each year sea ferries carry 33 million people in and out of the country, and 82 million come and go by air. The Channel Tunnel takes trains, cars, lorries and people under the sea and connects the UK with the rest of Europe.

Gatwick is one of the world's busiest airports.

Communications

Because of its small size the United Kingdom has always had many advanced ways of sending messages and information from place to place. In 1840 Britain had the first organised postal system, the Penny Post. In 1936 the world's first high-definition public television service was introduced by the BBC.

Television pictures and phone messages from all over the world can be sent directly into people's homes via satellites up in space or through cables laid under the ground.

1840
Penny Post

Calling for help

Can you find the person calling for an ambulance?

The 999 call made on the mobile phone is picked up by a nearby aerial and passes through the phone system to the control centre for the emergency services. From here the information is radioed to the ambulance nearest the scene of the accident. Some ambulances have computer screens on board to tell them where to go.

1922
First BBC radio broadcast

1936
First TV service

Mobile phones allow people to talk to each other through a special system of radio links.

1967
First colour TV service

1984
Sky satellite TV

How many different ways of sending a message can you find in the picture?

The Post Office handles over sixty million letters a day.

Computers in homes, offices and schools can send and receive information down the phone line.

The overhead copper wires that used to carry telephone messages are being replaced by 2 million kilometres of microwave links and optical fibres.

The latest technology allows people to communicate with each other quicker than ever before.

Energy and power

Each year more and more energy is consumed in the United Kingdom by industry and people at home. Different fuels are better at different things.

Coal, gas and oil are burned to produce heat. These fuels are used in fires and boilers to heat homes, offices and factories. Power stations turn heat into electricity, which is then used for lighting or to work machines. Oil can be turned into petrol to drive motor vehicles.

Coal

Coal-fired power stations once produced nearly all the UK's electricity. Many of these stations have now closed down, because smoke from burning coal pollutes the atmosphere. Also, the government does not want to rely on the miners who dig the coal from the ground and the train drivers who deliver it to the stations.

Coal-fired power station, Yorkshire

Hinkley Point nuclear power station, Somerset

North Sea oil

Gas and oil were first brought ashore from under the North Sea in 1975. Before this, the UK imported most of its oil and made gas by burning coal. Now the UK is the world's ninth largest producer of oil and the fifth largest producer of gas. It exports these fuels to other countries.

Nuclear power

Less than a quarter of the UK's electricity comes from nuclear power stations. These are built on the coast so the sea water can be used to keep the machinery cool. Although nuclear power stations do not produce smoke from chimneys, many people are worried about the effects of radioactive waste in years to come.

Laggan Dam, Scotland

Hydro-electric power

Hydro-electric power plants use water to generate electricity. The natural flow of a river is held back by a dam. The water is then forced to flow through turbines to generate electricity. Nearly all the UK's hydro-electric plants are in Scotland. Half of them are on rivers that feed into the River Tay.

Sun, wind and waves

There are a few schemes in the UK that produce electricity using the heat of the sun or the power of the wind or waves. At the moment they contribute little to the country's energy needs. Even these environmentally friendly methods have an impact on the landscape. Large windmills need to be built on exposed and windswept hills, and tidal barrages may affect wildlife along the coast.

Percentage of UK electricity made by different fuels

- oil
- coal
- natural gas
- nuclear power
- hydro
- imported electricity

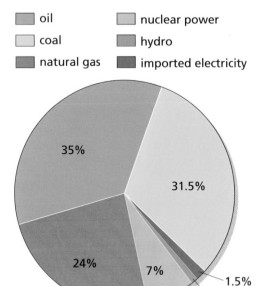

35%
31.5%
24%
7%
1.5%
1%

Wind turbines, West Yorkshire

A country village

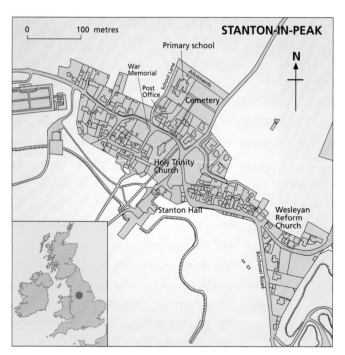

Look at the map and try to find the things shown in the photograph.

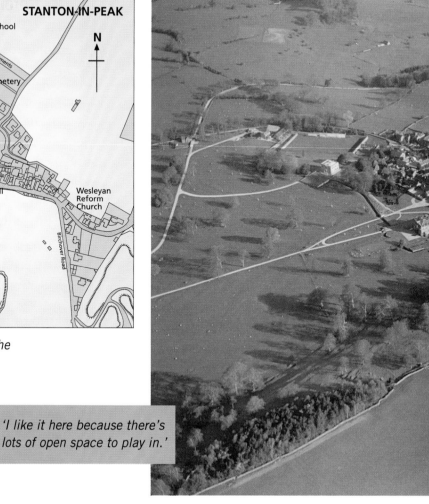

'I like it here because there's lots of open space to play in.'

Aerial view of Stanton-in-Peak, Derbyshire

Stanton-in-Peak is a village in the Pennine hills of Derbyshire. About 350 people live there. The village has a primary school, a few local shops and an infrequent bus service to the nearby town.

A village is a small settlement in the countryside. The number of people who live in a village can be as few as fifty or as many as a few thousand. In the past a village was home to all the people who worked on the surrounding land. Some villages belonged to a local landowner and were built close to his grand country home, where people in the village worked as domestic staff.

Today there are few jobs on the land and in domestic service. Many people who live in villages are retired or travel to nearby towns to work. Some villages have small industries or are pretty enough to attract tourists. This provides work for local people.

The problem for many villages is that if people move away or use their cars to shop in the town, then the local shop, garage or school may have to close down. There is only one class in some village schools.

'I don't like it here because you can't buy what you want at the little shop.'

Villages around the UK

Villages look different around the UK. In most parts of England the buildings are clustered around a central area, such as a village green or a pond. In Northern Ireland they are often in a line, along a road or at a crossroads. In parts of the Scottish Highlands a village marked on the map is actually separate houses scattered over the hillside with their own plots of land.

'I don't like it here because the nearest cinema is an hour's drive away.'

'I like it because you know everybody else who lives here.'

What might you find in a village?
- Small shops, such as a newsagent's, grocer's or sub-post office
- Public house (pub)
- Church or chapel
- Village hall
- Primary school
- Small garage or petrol station
- Doctor
- Bus stop, although the buses may not come very often, perhaps only once a week

Stone houses in the village of Stanton-in-Peak

A market town

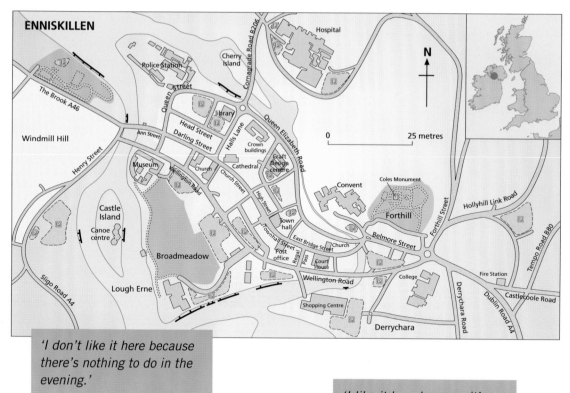

ENNISKILLEN

0   25 metres

'I don't like it here because there's nothing to do in the evening.'

'I like it here because it's small enough to know people and big enough to have lots of friends.'

Enniskillen is a market town in the county of Fermanagh in Northern Ireland. About ten thousand people live there. Most market towns were originally just that: markets where people came together to buy and sell their produce.

Farmers came from miles around to sell animals, fruit, vegetables, corn and wheat at the weekly market. Waiting to buy their produce were animal dealers, shopkeepers, corn merchants and other farmers. There were also open market stalls selling clothes, tools, household items and much more to the farmers and their families.

This still happens in Enniskillen today. The sheep are no longer driven down the wide main street and the cattle market has moved to a new building on the edge of town, but market day continues to be a scene of great bustle and activity. As well as the open market stalls, there is now a large supermarket.

The problem for many market towns is that more and more farmers no longer need to go to market because they sell direct to the large supermarket chains. Also, out-of-town shopping centres take business away from the small shops in the town centre.

The building with the tower is the town hall in Enniskillen. Look at the map and try to work out where this photograph was taken.

CHURCH ST. ENNISKILLEN. 3396. W.L.

What differences can you see between Enniskillen High Street in 1901 (top picture) and today (bottom picture)?

What might you find in a market town?

• Agricultural machinery, tractor and car showrooms for local farmers

• Auctioneers, estate agents and solicitors to buy and sell land, houses, farms and furniture

• Banks where people keep their money

• Pubs and hotels to meet friends, have a meal, clinch a deal or celebrate over a drink

• Secondary school for children from the surrounding village primary schools

• Bus station and taxi companies

• Doctors, dentists and a hospital

• Sports or leisure centre

• Railway station

An industrial city

Stoke-on-Trent is in Staffordshire in the English Midlands. It is home to 250 000 people. Stoke grew up in Victorian times because of the pottery industry which used the local clay and coal. Smoky factories were surrounded by terraced houses for the workers, schools and grand public buildings, such as town halls and libraries.

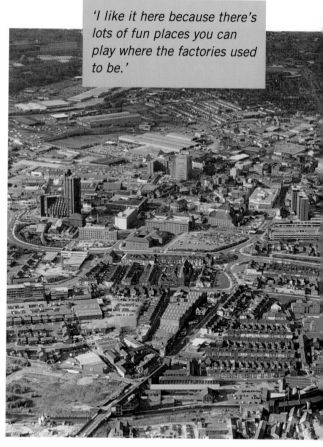

'I like it here because there's lots of fun places you can play where the factories used to be.'

Aerial view of the city centre, Stoke-on-Trent

Look at the map and try to find the things shown in the photograph.

Although the pottery industry is still doing well, many factories closed down in the 1960s. Thousands of working men and women lost their jobs and vast areas of the city became derelict. What has been done to help? Millions of pounds have been spent turning the old industrial landscape into parkland and open spaces. Marl holes created by digging clay from the ground have now been turned into lakes. The coal tips have become grassy hills. The old railway tracks are 'greenways' for walkers and cyclists, and the air is cleaner.

What might you find in an industrial city?

- Old terraced houses and new housing estates
- Old and new factories
- Local government offices and a town hall
- Library and museum
- Concert hall or theatre
- Shopping centres with well-known stores
- Choice of pubs, restaurants and hotels
- Choice of secondary schools and colleges, and perhaps a university
- Large hospital
- A national football or rugby team
- Inter-City railway station

'I don't like it here because the houses are old and cramped.'

Bottle-shaped kilns for making pottery in the city of Stoke, 1946

'I like it here because houses and things in the shops are cheap to buy.'

'I don't like living here because no one has heard of Stoke-on-Trent!'

New industries have come to the city. A business park has been built on the site of an old blast furnace. Discount stores and a ten-screen cinema stand where there was once a coal mine. A grimy slurry lagoon has become a marina for canal boats. New offices and a luxury hotel have also been built. The people of Stoke-on-Trent would not have dreamt of having these things in their city thirty years ago.

Although new jobs have been created they are not suitable for many people who lost their jobs when the old industries closed down. Few steelworkers or miners get jobs behind the supermarket check-outs or in the building society offices, but their wives, daughters and sons do.

The pottery industry still makes its famous dinner sets, decorated figures, tiles and industrial ceramics. It now uses more modern methods and employs fewer people.

Wedgwood china made in Stoke-on-Trent

A new town

In 1968 the Government decided to expand the small town of Peterborough into a new town. The idea was to provide somewhere for people to move to from overcrowded London, 80 miles to the south.

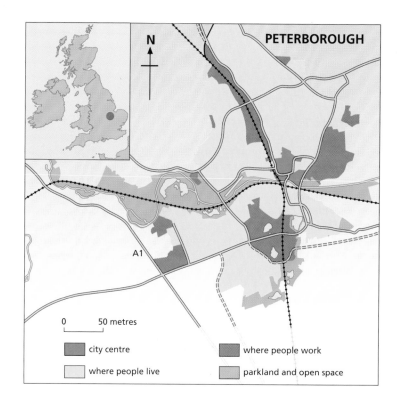

Peterborough has a planned system of cycleways.

The new town was planned with separate zones for housing, shopping, industry, business and leisure. A new road system was built with 'parkways' to speed traffic round the city, keeping cars away from the areas where people live. Access by car was made difficult on purpose.

Only on foot or by bike can people easily get around the residential areas and to the local shopping centres. Peterborough has one of the largest cycling systems in the UK. It has 140 kilometres (87 miles) of cycleways which link shops, homes and schools and avoid busy roads.

The population of Peterborough is now 150 000, three times what it was before the new town was built. Many well-known companies have moved to the city from other parts of the country and built new offices in the landscaped countryside.

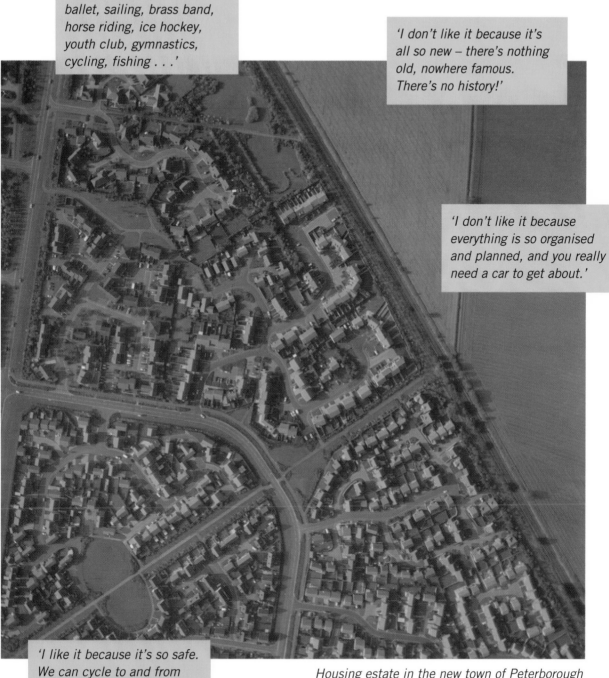

'I like it because there are so many things I can do – ballet, sailing, brass band, horse riding, ice hockey, youth club, gymnastics, cycling, fishing . . .'

'I don't like it because it's all so new – there's nothing old, nowhere famous. There's no history!'

'I don't like it because everything is so organised and planned, and you really need a car to get about.'

'I like it because it's so safe. We can cycle to and from school by ourselves and no one worries, and my parents can drive to work in a few minutes.'

Housing estate in the new town of Peterborough

A holiday resort

Tenby is a seaside resort on the south coast of Pembrokeshire in Wales. The weather in Tenby is mild and sunny because the coast is sheltered from the prevailing south-westerly winds and is warmed by the waters of the Gulf Stream.

About a hundred ago people started coming to Tenby by train from the industrial towns of South Wales and the English Midlands. They came to enjoy a day on the beach. People still do this today, although most of them now travel by coach or car.

A 1940s railway poster advertising Tenby as a holiday destination

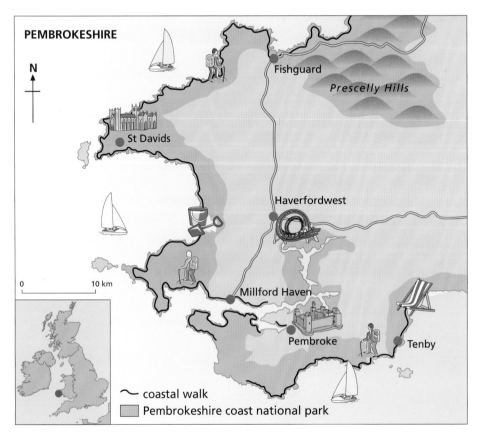

Oakwood theme park near Haverfordwest

Holiday weather

About a million visitors a year come to Pembrokeshire for the beaches and dramatic coastal scenery. Like any holiday resort, a lot depends on the weather.

In Pembrokeshire the weather is temperate with few extremes of hot or cold. The coast itself is quite dry because the clouds, blown by the wind from the south-west, drop most of their rain on the hills inland.

The mild climate is good for outdoor activities such as sunbathing, surfing, swimming in the sea, walking along the coastal path, pony trekking in the hills, sailing round the coast and climbing the cliffs. Even the wet and windswept Prescelly Hills are ideal for an exhilarating walk with wonderful views, as long as you wrap up warm!

If the weather does turn nasty, Pembrokeshire has fine historic buildings to explore, such as St David's Cathedral and Pembroke Castle.

Canoeing off the Pembrokeshire coast

Seaports

Because the United Kingdom is made up of islands it has always relied on trade coming in and out of its seaports. Today three-quarters of overseas trade comes and goes by sea. Over thirty million passengers a year travel in and out of the UK by sea, mostly on ferries to and from the rest of Europe.

N

Sullom Voe
Lerwick

Scrabster

Fraserburgh
Peterhead
Aberdeen

Dundee
Oban
Finnart
Forth
Glasgow
Ardrossan

0   100 km
0   50 miles

Larne
Carrickfergus
Belfast

Stranraer

Tyne
Tees and Hartlepool
Scarborough

Fleetwood
Hull

Liverpool
Holyhead
Garston
Ellesmere Port

Grimsby and Immingh
Boston

Great Yarmouth

Fishguard

Felixstowe

Milford Haven

Canvey Island   Ha

Avonmouth
London
Ra
Portsmouth
Dov

Poole
Padstow
Weymouth
Southampton

Newlyn
Plymouth
Falmouth

Types of port

- passenger
- oil
- container
- fishing
- naval

Fishing ports

From fishing ports around the UK over 11 000 fishing boats catch more than 600 000 tonnes of fish each year. That's more than half the fish we eat. The main fishing ports are on the east coast of Scotland, such as Aberdeen, Peterhead and Fraserburgh.

For centuries the Royal Navy has had shipyards round the coast to patrol the seas and defend the UK against its enemies. Naval ports include Portsmouth, Plymouth, Portland, Rosyth and Chatham.

Until the 1960s nearly everything was loaded on and off ships by crane and by hand. Today most ports handle goods, such as iron ore and wheat, in bulk and fill a whole ship with the same thing. Many other ships carry cargo in easy-to-handle containers which come straight off the ship and onto a lorry.

In the past the busiest UK ports were those facing west towards America, such as Liverpool. Now ports facing east towards Europe handle most trade. The Port of London has nearly 50 million tonnes pass through it each year.

UK top five ports
★ London

★ Tees and Hartlepool

★ Sullom Voe

★ Grimsby and Immingham

★ Milford Haven

Goods being unloaded by hand in Glasgow, 1945

Tanker (left) loading crude oil at Sullom Voe, Shetland Islands

Milford Haven in West Wales and Sullom Voe in the Shetlands are only small towns where few people live, but between them they handle 75 million tonnes of oil each year. The oil comes and goes in huge tankers or by pipeline.

Dover, in the south-east of England, is the closest point to France. This is the most important port in the UK for roll-on roll-off traffic. Trucks and cars can drive straight on and off the cross-channel ferries and be in France in just over an hour.

Capital cities

The United Kingdom has four capital cities. Edinburgh is the capital of Scotland, Cardiff is the capital of Wales, Belfast is the capital of Northern Ireland and London is the capital of England.

Edinburgh

Edinburgh castle, built on a rocky outcrop, was the ancient home of the Scottish kings. The elegant new town, built in the eighteenth century, has streets of Georgian houses made of sandstone. Edinburgh has a great tradition of education, with a university, museums and art galleries.

View of Edinburgh from Calton Hill

Cardiff's grand civic centre

Cardiff

Although Cardiff has a Norman castle at its centre, the city grew up in Victorian times as a port to export coal from the mining valleys of South Wales. It has a grand civic centre, with university buildings and museums. Cardiff was not officially made the capital of Wales until 1955, making it the UK's youngest capital city.

How many people live there?
- Greater London   7 million
- Edinburgh   440 thousand
- Cardiff   296 thousand
- Belfast   289 thousand

Belfast

Originally built at a crossing on the River Lagan, Belfast grew into the biggest shipbuilding city in the world. That was a hundred years ago. Today the city has a busy shopping centre and a new concert hall where the docks used to be. Over half the people in Northern Ireland live in the city of Belfast.

Castle Court shopping centre in Belfast

London

London is the capital of England and the United Kingdom. Greater London covers over 3000 square kilometres and has a population of seven million. It is a major world centre for finance, tourism, newspapers and broadcasting.

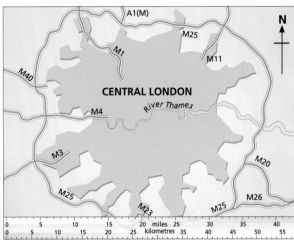

The Houses of Parliament in London are the centre of UK government and a tourist attraction.

Half the money spent in the UK by overseas tourists is spent in London. The nation's government is based there, and 750 million passenger journeys a year are made on the London Underground – that's the same number as on the whole of the British Rail system. London has some of the most expensive houses in the country, and also the greatest number of homeless people.

There is conflict between all the different things that go on in London at the same time. Cars battle with local buses, who struggle for road space with delivery vans. Cyclists squeeze past forty-tonne trucks, while tourists fight for space with people who are trying to get to work.

Environmental issues

Many people in the United Kingdom are worried about the impact of modern living on the environment. Almost everything that improves life for one person spoils it for someone else.

Issue	For	Against
Fertilisers and chemicals used in modern farming methods	Produce crops that are bigger, cheaper and free of disease.	Wildlife is affected and rivers are polluted. People worry about the safety of their food.
Farm animals reared in large sheds	Animals are kept under controlled conditions and are protected from the weather to produce the best meat.	Animals have no freedom to move about in the open air.
Factories	Employ people to make useful things.	Use up raw materials, create pollution and dump industrial waste in rivers.
Quarrying and mining	Only source of coal and stone.	Spoils the countryside, and uses up a non-renewable resource.
More roads for cars and lorries	People can travel to more places. Goods are transported quickly and efficiently around the country.	Exhaust gases pollute the air. Difficult for people, especially children, to get about safely. Public transport becomes worse.
Packaging	Protects delicate products such as food and hi-fi equipment.	Difficult to get rid of waste. Creates litter.
Out-of-town shopping centres	Shoppers can buy everything they want in one visit at cheaper prices.	People need cars to get to and from shops. Small shops in town centres close down.
More electricity and power	Electricity keeps homes warm (and offices cool) and works things such as TVs and washing machines.	Waste gases from power stations pollute the atmosphere and cause acid rain. People are worried about nuclear power. North Sea oil will not last for ever.
New houses, offices and shopping centres	People need homes to live in and pleasant places to work and shop.	Building uses up valuable land and spoils the countryside.
Tourism	People enjoy visiting beautiful places and historic buildings.	Too many people can spoil the beauty of the place they have come to see.
Fewer people working	More leisure time for people to do what they want.	More unemployment, so people have less money to spend.

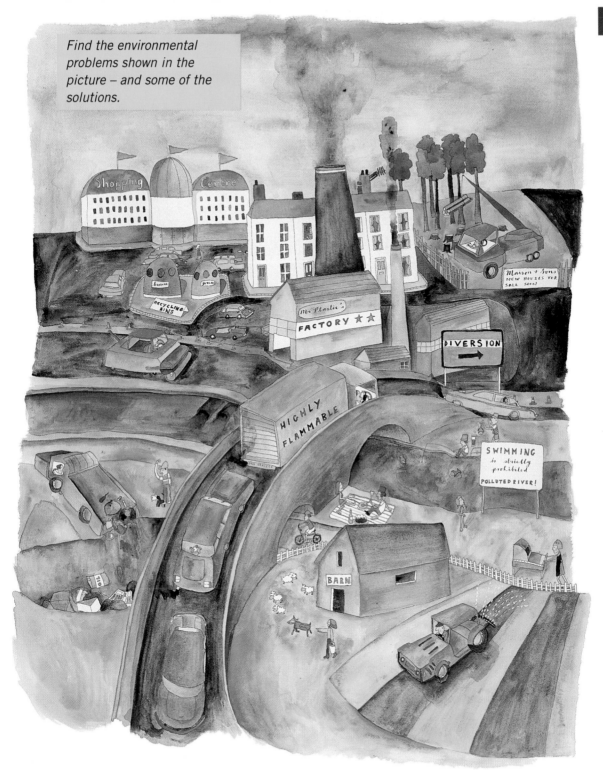

Find the environmental problems shown in the picture – and some of the solutions.

To be kinder to the environment, people have to make changes to the way that they live. Organic farming methods do less damage to land, produce less pollution and give us healthier food. But the food costs more to buy.

Land reclamation schemes turn derelict land into open spaces. Traffic schemes keep out cars, encouraging pedestrians and cyclists and improving public transport. Recycling rubbish saves raw materials and energy.

Looking to the future

Since 1973 the United Kingdom has been part of the European Union. The countries of Europe who joined the European Union work together to encourage trade between their countries and to share the same plans for the future.

Countries of the European Union

Looking to Europe

The UK already has close ties with other countries in the European Union.

• It is easy to get from the UK to the rest of Europe. There are frequent cross-channel ferries.

• There are direct rail connections between UK cities and other cities in Europe through the Channel Tunnel.

• Over a quarter of the UK population takes their holidays in Europe.

• People can travel freely and work in any other country in the European Union.

• Truck-loads of goods travel without hold-ups at borders. This encourages trade between European countries.

• Children have the right to go to school in any other European Union country.

• People in the UK can elect Members to the European Parliament.

• There are plans for similar laws and a shared currency for all countries in the European Union.

Looking to the world

It is now easier than ever before to travel from the UK and see the world. Worldwide television and newspaper reports bring events around the world into our homes. Satellite communications allow us to talk to other countries. We can find out what is happening everywhere. A disaster in one place, such as global warming, a nuclear accident or a war, can affect us all. World problems are now everyone's problems.

Looking to the UK

In the past fifty years there have been many improvements to people's lives in the UK. People now live longer earn more money and have more possessions. However, these improvements are not shared equally. The richest one-tenth of the UK population owns half the wealth. While many people are better off, with well-paid jobs and comfortable homes, some are worse off, with no job, no money and nowhere to live. Many people eat better food and are healthier than before, while others eat poorly and suffer illness. Although many people have family and friends to look after them when they are old or ill, others have no one.

Homeless people sell the magazine The Big Issue in the streets to make some money.

The Queen and President Mitterand of France arrive at Folkstone in Le Shuttle, after the opening of the Channel Tunnel on 6 May 1994.

Index

Published by BBC Educational Publishing, a division of BBC Education, BBC White City, 201 Wood Lane, London W12 7TS

First published 1996

© Peter Evans/BBC Education 1996

The moral right of the author has been asserted.

Paperback ISBN: 0 563 37276 1
Hardback ISBN: 0 563 37275 3

Colour reproduction by Daylight, Singapore
Printed by BPC

Photo credits: The British Petroleum Company Plc **p. 41** (**bottom**); Cardiff Marketing Ltd **p. 42** (**right**); Environmental Picture Library **p. 28** (**bottom**); Luke Finn/BBC Education **p. 13**; Format Partners Photo Library **p. 7** (**top and bottom left**); Freemans **p. 25** (**top**); Robert Harding Picture Library **pp. 7** (**bottom right**), 16, 23 (**top**), 43 (**bottom**); Holt Studios **p. 21**; Hulton Deutsch Collection **pp. 11** (**bottom**), 14 (**top**), 35 (**top**); Images Colour Library **p. 23** (**bottom**), 28 (**top**), 29 (**bottom**); David Jones **p. 31** (**bottom**); Greater Manchester Metro Ltd **p. 25** (**bottom left**); Museum of London **p. 14** (**bottom**) *Frost Fair by Hondius*; National Museum of Ireland **p. 33**; National Museums and Galleries on Merseyside, Walker Art Gallery **p. 10** *Henry VIII by Hans Eworth*; National Portrait Gallery, London **p. 11** (**top**) *Elizabeth I by Marcus Gheeraerts*; National Trust Photographic Library **p. 15** (**top**); Network **p. 22**; Northern Ireland Tourist Board **p. 43** (**top**); Nunn Syndication **p. 4**; Oakwood Leisure Ltd **p. 39** (**top**); Greater Peterborough Partnership **p. 36**; Photoair **pp. 30/31, 34/35, 37**; Popperfoto **p. 41** (**top**); Quadrant Picture Library **p. 25** (**middle and bottom right**); Rex Features **pp. 7** (**top right**), 15 (**bottom**), 47; Science and Society Picture Library **p. 38**; Scotland in Focus **pp. 2** (**bottom**), 29 (**top**), 42 (**left**); Scottish Highland Photo Library **p. 6** (**left**); Spectrum Colour Library **pp. 2** (**top**), 9, 18 (**top**); Twr-y-Felin Outdoor Centre **p. 39** (**bottom**); John Walmsley **p. 6** (**right**); Waterways Photo Library/Derek Pratt **p. 18** (**bottom**); Wedgwood **p. 35** (**bottom**).

Illustrations: © Nila Aye, 1996 (pages 26-27, 45); © Hardlines, 1996 (pages 3,4, 5, 6, 12,20,21, 24, 25, 29, 30, 32, 34, 36, 38, 40, 42, 43); © Michael Munday, 1996 (pages 8-9, 17, 18-19, 46).

Front cover: Science Photo Library (**main picture**) *satellite image of the United Kingdom*; Tony Stone Images (**right**) *rollercoaster ride*.